Studies of Life
A Collection of

Poetry
Love Sonnets
&
Thoughts

By
Lauresa Tomlinson
Larry Tomlinson

All rights reserved. No part of this book may be reproduced, stored in a retrieval system or transited in any form or by any means without the prior written permission, except by a professional reviewer who may quote a brief passage in a review to be printed in a newspaper, magazine, journal or online reviews.

Zjavanee Publications
P.O. Box 2274
McKinville, CA 95519

2017

Afraid to Look

People getting drunk or drugged thinking they can
get close to or run from their true thoughts

Afraid to see their life as it really is

Feeling trapped by society and other expectations

Fear of letting others down if they
become who they really are

Some people see life easier if they go along,
rather than making waves

Be happy with what you're given,
The one who marches to another's drum usually
gets lost

Why not dance to your own music
If it doesn't harm anyone else
Don't hide who you are, be proud.

by
Lauresa Tomlinson
5/2/91

Alien

Just a misguided alien come here to play
with funny looks and weird ways looking to stay

Blending right in with the colored hair and
wuzy dress and who gives a care
Just come to play and I just might stay

See what's going on here and beyond
To see if the way is won or just begun

Been to the stars and past
But here's the best show to cast
Just come to play and just might stay

by
Lauresa Tomlinson
1986
This was written as a song but the music has been lost

All Began as One

Man was created as one with nature
but has drifted apart.
Now the nature of all is calling
for that unity once again.
Join the freedom call,
the call is going out to all.
All who answers truly become free.
Free to fly, to be all they can be.
Answer the call, Answer it Now,
Don't wait, Fly, and be free.
See all for what it is. Free.
Freedom to build,
Freedom to help and to BE

by
Lauresa Tomlinson
9/28/94
inspired by music

Because

Because you are the Lord of my hopes and dreams
Because you are the keeper of my strength
Because you are the Watcher of my ways and my path
Because you are the Healer of my crisis and my screams

I love you Father God, Keeper of my life
I love you oh Guard of my nights and my days
I love you oh my Strength and Remover of my Strife

Forgive me, my Father for being weak
Forgive me oh Keeper of my Soul
I give my all to you oh Father of my heart and every beat

You, oh Father God are my Strength, my love, life my all

by
Lauresa Tomlinson
1987

Cry Out Oh Heavens

Clap your hand oh great thunder
Be thou the attention-getter of man
Weep then because of the destruction man
has caused to the Creator's great wonders.

For of all God's creations man is the most destructive.
With his struggle for power and his ever-growing ego,
Like a child, thinking he is smarter than all the teachers,
Man is gaining in ego and lacking in wisdom.

Man has power over all of God's creation but
only when used in the right way.
A puzzle is not completed with the pieces of another puzzle,
the picture's not the same.

So weep oh clouds that the attention of man will be gained
before the destruction of all he knows
Cry out oh heavens and awaken man to One
even more powerful than himself.

by
Lauresa Tomlinson
9/04

Calling for Help

Come winds eternal, blow away the dullness
of man's mind.
Awaken him to the knowledge of the All.
Let him awaken to the true nature of being and
not be so blind.

Blow oh winds of knowing, help man
grow in wisdom.
To live together in the harmony of oneness.
To be the beings of love and
the knowing that we are of the one sum.

Shine oh Son of The Most High,
that man might know Spirit and be tall.
With the mighty sword, clip at the bud of the Ego
That man not stumble and fall but
live strong in the knowledge of it all.

Come oh Holy rains that man's body might
grow straight and strong.
That his mind grasps the clearness of it all, and
becomes the joy and love of the one
who does no wrong.

As knowledge opens to man and
he learns to live, love and create,
He will grow to be the child he was meant to be.
To live the plan as from the beginning,
to live and love without fear and hate.

Calling For Help   con't

As we learn to live in harmony
without fear and hate leading the way,
we will build a future so bright,
that the stars may dim in its light as we
make a brighter day.

by
Lauresa Tomlinson
8/3/2004

Dance The Dance

As the dance of life goes on and on
Some see it as fun and good
Some see it as serious, full of lessons

Dance on my friend, dance on
See, look ahead, see with your heart,
Look into your mind
See the dream, see it whole and not apart

You are now the creator of your fame
You do it now, willing or not
You're the creative force in your life's fame

Live it full, full of life
Live it good, live it strong
Live it free of strife.

Dance in step with the Creators beat

by
Lauresa Tomlinson
9/28/94
inspired while listening to music

Each Day Anew

Each day starts with a bitter cold that numbs the Soul.

Your light shining forth has warmth

and brings forth the blossoms.

It burns away the clouds of darkness

that drifts through the heavens

carrying the tears of times past.

I love you oh splendid twinkle,

when eternity is unfolding.

For without your spark, all would be dark.

So shine on. So I may start my every day a new!

By
Laurence Tomlinson
1983

Eons Past on

How easy it is sometimes to forget the past
Eons ago places past and sometimes forgotten
like dreams tossed in the wind –
drifting without a care.

Temples of Peace and Power sparkling in their glory
Sparkling as crystals shimmering as gold as
lustrous as pearls - marvelous as diamonds
Singing in harmony with the Universe,
when animals and man could talk as one
and all lived side by side in peace
seeking the good of all

How quick we forget the good and
the love felt by all that has passed this way.
How real the bad becomes when dwelled in.
Reach for that day when as eons ago, man
and all creation lived, played, loved
and shared all that was.

When all was given free and never asked for in return,
When harmony and peace was always felt.
When ego was of not.
When power was not sought and all were free to fly
and all could feel without judgment and fear.

Oh what a glorious day again
We will reach when we seek
Thy Holy Will

By
Lauresa Tomlinson
4/26/88 original

Falling In Love

I felt so down and blue until I knew
that the twinkle in your eye was for me,
And my heart would make me warm with that clue.

Our Love deepens every day as we play.
We share and care and this helps our love grow,
We walk and talk and this helps it stay.

With Love in our hearts and smiles on our faces
We can challenge the world together and win,
for together as one we can really go places.

by
Lauresa Tomlinson
1/8/03

Freedom at Last or Silent Screams

As I sit and think all closed in a box,
of the things, I've done and gained forgiveness for all.

Awaiting the arrival of the next Karmic box
I sit alone in myself with my silent screams

To find a way to be set free, to find that key
To forgive and be forgiven- to make amends.

Yes, Yes! I know that key - now to reach
and touch that key before all is swept away.

To know and release, to be released
I know, I know - touch, touch it now,
How I cry, How do I touch it, just out of grasp.

To release all and let it go - that's the key-
That's the key - ah, so easy, but yet so hard -
I know if happiness is really mine it will come back.

by
Lauresa Tomlinson
5/3/91

Getting High

Getting high isn't taking drugs,
getting high is waking in the morning,
feeling you beside me.

Seeing the sunlight in your eyes and love on your lips.
Knowing you will always be near when I need help
and when failure comes,
knowing our love for each other and
our faith will see us through till the sun shines again.

Getting high is knowing I have you to share all of my
life with.
Not just the ups but someone who cares when things
are low.
Knowing I just have to be me and always be loved.

by
Lauresa Tomlinson
12/16/09

Freedom to Fly

Freedom is yours, Freedom is mine
Feel it, Feel it
Free to fly, Free, Free to be kind

Love it, Fly, Fly high
Nature is all free,
We are Free
Be free, Free to create, Free to fly

To be free to flow with the winds,
To be free to fly with the soaring,
To be free to blend with snow
As it drifts softly to the earth

And yet be free to dance in the rain
To dance in the free falls of water
Free to create the best and beautiful

Look and see the wonders of freedom
To look with your inner heart
Feel it with your being

Love it with your wholeness
Being one with all and see as one
The goal is what?

Being one with all that is natural
The goals that we set, is it before
Or after we are here?

Freedom to Fly con't

Were those goals for self-gain and enjoyment?
Or for power and ego?
Or were they things to help?
Set man free to gain the good of all
and Not for the good of one?

In what mind frame did man come
It amazes me that the human race
Has lasted as long as it has

So much power is taken and
Given to the ego types
and the small-minded.
We have all but forgotten our Father
The One who gave us this life
To weave as we will, take a long look
Are you all that you hoped for.
Is it time to let go and get help

By
Lauresa Tomlinson
9/28/94 inspired by music

How Far

The beauty of the past is not all lost

But how far will we allow it to fade?

To reach for the beauty and to live its
essence is to be our goal

To learn and finally grasp the wisdoms
that are waiting

To understand what the universe is
teaching before it's too late to save it.

By
Lauresa Tomlinson
1990's

Just for you

Just look at who you have surrounding
you with their love

Look up what do you see?
Billowy white clouds floating by smiling just at you

Let the sunshine through and see the light of love

Beautiful blue skies watching with love held high

Around you wondrous trees sway with
gentle songs of love just for you.

Marvelous flowers of various colors and
sweetness dance to love's song just for you.

Luscious green grasses sparkle like diamonds with
dew showing their shimmering love, just for you.

All these things have The Creator made for your
enjoyment,
Just to love you the more.

Sing along with them the song of love, enjoy,
become as one.

By
Lauresa Tomlinson
5/12/88

In The Beginning

In the beginning and yet before humankind,
The Creator was dancing with
everything upon the Earth,
Delighting in the creation and splendor thereof.

Then being inspired with the idea of creating
yet another set of beings that could think
and could take care of all precious things that had
been created.

The Creator sat and worked out all the quirks
that could be found right away
in the design needed for this planet.

So humankind was created with two of almost
everything: two hands, feet, legs, arms,
eyes, ears, lungs, kidneys and
even two halves of a brain.

And with all this, The Creator wished for it to be used
to keep this wondrous place whole and
in working order.

Soon after creating humankind,
The Creator went on to create other places of beauty.
Leaving humankind in charge of the Earth
and leaving with them the power over all the plants,
creatures and weather,
believing that all would be well.

In The Beginning con't

The Creator soon found that most of humankind
had a flaw and had become lazy
and uncaring even for its own young.

They cared about nothing
except their own needs for the moment.
But there were a few that cared but they had to fight
with everything they thought they had,
to protect what was left of the splendid creation
The Creator had put in their trust.

But even these had forgotten the power
The Creator had left them in charge of
and the uncaring had stolen it away to a secret place.

Where only the thoughtless law-keepers could use it
to their own advantages.

So from the heart of The Creator was created a High
Being that would come to Earth,
to teach humankind once again about their power
and how to protect all that was created from the
beginning.

All the Creatures and plants great and small-
some seen and some unseen, some so small that
humankind's awareness cannot conceive them.

In The Beginning   con't

All was created with a purpose,
Some for beauty and pleasant to the eye,
Some for flavor and tantalizing to the taste,
Some for texture and invigorating to the touch,
Some for thought and enlightening to the mind,
Some for Spiritual awareness and
rejuvenating to the soul,

Some for healing and fitting for the body,
Some so small and yet so powerful,
to hold the breath of humankind.

But alas, humankind in the dullness of mind
and uncaring of the will, have destroyed themselves
through neglect and selfishness.

Oh, humankind, now with your pockets full of
precious metals...
Where do you perceive to go?
What next do you care to destroy?

Us, The Children of The Universe, say NO!
Not Here! No, Not There!

Stay on Earth, the small once blue planet glistening
with life and wonder of love.
Stay on your now gray dying world
and watch her sleep
the sleep of death and dream the dream of chaos.

In The Beginning con't

What good is your gold in that?
Does it bring you life,
happiness, health, or spirituality?
No...., for this all comes from a loving heart.

Only through love and caring for your
Mother Planet will you live.
Love your neighbor, be they creatures, plants,
mineral or humankind, large or small,
from your own planet or another of
The Creator's creations.

Through this only, will you gain your true freedom.
We, All will be watching.
We are waiting.

For there are a few of you that are learning
the truths and freedoms that come
with being a Child of The Universe.

Use your powers to heal all
and be happy with all that is.
But quicken your pace for your Mother's time is short.

Unless more of you join
in The Universal Plan of love and freedom,
like others of The Creators children have,
your planet will lose its place.

Let this love show you the peace, joy
and freedom we exist in now and forever.

by
Ma Sri Zjavanee/ Lauresa Tomlinson
6/19/96

Just One

Sailing in the skies
One with The Father
How wonderful not to mind time

One with Him who created all
Never to grow old
Always to feel loved
Never to feel old

One with all
Always free - Just to be
Always me and one

Happy with the Father
Sadness is gone
No more pain to bother
Always free - Just to be one.

By
Lauresa Tomlinson
5/13/88

Know Yourself

To know your linage and who you are-

To know the people you represent and
what they stood for.

To know the old ones and the
knowledge they have or had.

To respect the old ones and their ways-

To respect them and yourself and to show the
world that they live on in spirit even if not in flesh.

To show them respect by your thoughts,
your actions and in your way of life.

By respecting your people and loving
yourself for who you are
You gain that same respect from
others who know you.

Through that respect, you know
you are important to others.

Love and know yourself

by
Lauresa Tomlinson
10/30/90

Knowing

     From time eternal and into the recesses of man's mind does The Creator dwell.
     To spring upon man the evolution of time that knowledge of truth, be known to all that none should parish but to live forever to become one with him from whom all wisdom springs
     That all should know the face of The Creator and all power is given that all shall regain with him forever in peace, love and harmony

By
Lauresa Tomlinson
5/4/88

Lost Dreams

What goes on in a person's head when
They lose the vision they once had?
When that dream is washed away?

Dream another dream, you may say
But some only have one dream and
When it is gone, they want to leave and
go home or fade away.

Some can manage this by a piece at a time
and some just check out all at once

The ones that drift in pieces or sections
Die of a broken heart. The others that check
out all at once, commit death by selection.

Freedom is lost to both
Suicide is that of a quitter
and the other is one that gets lost along the way.

Are you a dreamer? or Dream Maker
If so, hold on with both hands!
Do it, Dream it big.

by
Lauresa Tomlinson
9/28/94
inspired by music

Past Wisdoms

To grasp the beautiful wisdoms of the past,
before they fade away and get lost.
How far will we allow them to fade?
Not to live them, not to keep and
use those wisdoms may be the cost.

To reach for that beauty and to live its essence is to be
our goal
To hold and live the treasured lessons of the Universe
To boldly know and show that fear has
no part to play in this role.

To move ahead into the future with the wisdoms that
we can understand is the greatest
part of life that one can give.
To teach the young to carry on into the new day,
as no one but they can.

So is the way of the bright new and
bold future of life that love is the clue.
To hold the hope of all things new, knowing
that the love and wisdom will always
shine in people like you.

by
Lauresa Tomlinson
8/03/2004

Lovers We Are

The flight of free lovers is love without the
boundaries of the physical body.

Lovers of all that is and was and
all that ever will be.

Lovers of ideas in movement from
moment to moment.

Lovers of space and time, lovers of love itself.

Ahh, to be a lover is the most awesome
dream one could have.

To love endless and unrestricted,
to touch all around with that universal high.

To love that highest love and
present it to mankind and all creation.

To help all feel that love of one and all,
nonconforming to the world's ideas on love.

Universally love is that which all seek and
very few know.

To feel that love without end,
that beautiful love of creation.

Lover of all, to be a lover of time and space,
to see all be one in love,
to feel that comfort and touch of a friend
without prejudice and evil.

Lovers We Are con't

Just to feel, just to know,
ahh, that feeling of being a lover of all.

Lovers of our own close loved ones

Bring lovers through time and space
Lovers of ourselves and others

Lovers of intelligence without
restrictions of form or face

Lovers of nature's ways

Lovers of feeling, inspiration, and ideas

Lovers from afar and near

Ahh, to love all without the worry of judgment

This is truly what love was meant to be.

by
Lauresa Tomlinson
7/25/89

Oh My Midnight

Sitting here by myself, alone,
Holding my arms around myself,
I can see so clearly now.

My mind is clear as the midnight sky above.
All my ideas and aspirations shinning as stars
on this starlit night.

Oh come now my midnight sky,
have one idea shine brighter than all the rest
Let me be able to focus on just one.

But no, they all twinkle the same
as does the problems of an artist.

Which one do I choose to show off?
Which one outshines the rest?
Is it this piece made of clay?

Is it this painting over here or over there?
Is it this piece I have poured my heart into
or that piece that holds my emotions so clearly?

Oh My Midnight   con't

Oh my midnight sky, how I need your help.
Pick one, just one, and let it shine for me this night.

My mind now so cluttered with the
shining stars of my hands, heart, and soul.
Which, I ask, should I focus my energy on.

And so it is when you can see things so clearly
that you understand that each of us has
a lot to give. But what should we give first?

Should it be of our hands,
our hearts or from our souls,
that others should enjoy.

by
Lauresa Tomlinson
12/23/09

Once Pure

The pure rays of light seeks a home,
a place of peace.

A place to become strong then off to fly again
leaving in its home the brilliant colors of a rainbow
as a sign to all that this is the home of a
pure ray of hope.

Seek to become that pure and peaceful radiant home
for the Son's ray of Holy Light, that all may see
and know one is here to help lead the way.

Pointing the gifts of the rainbow
in the direction of the Son,
that all may receive and become pure of heart,
soul and mind, to shine once again.

by
Lauresa Tomlinson
4/26/88

Questions oh Father

Oh my Holy Father I ask of Thee
keep me wholly n Thy will.
Help me Father never trespass against you,
and keep me in your sight.
Heal my questioned spirit -oh Father,
Thy Holy will be done in me.

Questions oh Father rise in my soul.
The West has said pray this way and
yet there is remorse felt.
My soul says, there is something missing.
The East says chant this way,
But Oh Father am I heard?

Is it wrong for one to pray in a way
that feels good to the soul?
In a way that is from the heart?
To pray from the heart using the body,
the mind and the tongues of the Heavenly Host?

Oh Holy Father questions arise and need answers.
How could praying, singing, dancing, and speaking
with the tongues of the Heavenly Host be wrong
when it makes the heart light and the soul fly free?
Yet when asking organized religion,
they say pray this way or that.

Oh Heavenly Father heed this child's
questioning heart.
Keep me in Thy Holy Will.

By
Lauresa Tomlinson
4/26/88

Really Seeing

To push beyond the muck and mire of mortal pain.

To go beyond the torturing anguish of the soul

To see with the free but sometimes
laden eyes of the soul

To go beyond -beyond I say,
those seeming barriers of time and space

To see over the next horizon is the dream
of all who know

To fly free and feel that freedom to your core.

To know that special freedom as your own.

This is what most seek and few realize.

That special Freedom was given by one alone.

The one and only that came from
on high to help.

Go beyond by holding the hand of the
Holy Creator's Son, Jesus

by
Lauresa Tomlinson
5/4/91

Searching

Sitting here under the midnight skies

Searching the heavens for my home

Feeling homesick and a longing to go back

and not to be alone.

Yet knowing that cannot be till I have

completed my challenges here

and know what I might see or find.

Oh what quiet and painful suffering to me

When is school over and what have I to learn or do?

Did I pass and can I move on or

is there yet more for me to learn

or is my passage earned?

When oh when I ask, may I go home?

By
Lauresa Tomlinson
4/26/88

Sands of Time

Through the sands of time and
all that man has known,
The winds can change all in a twinkle of the eye.

Though forceful the changes are many in
man's thoughts,
One thing exists through all.
The creative force of all is ever-changing,
never stopping, ever creating anew

Man with his mind so small, thinking he is mighty,
is fast to anger, thinking to conquer all,
can be beaten even by the air he depends on.

Through the eons of time,
man has grown and then fallen,
Then outgrown himself once again
growing destructive,

Yet the timeless winds stand by awaiting the mighty
command that changes all,

Once again creating anew with hopes
That man will love life more than power.

Once man learns this timeless lesson,
then man and creation can live,
love and grow into ultimate happiness,
with plenty of time and energy to learn.

Sands of Time (con't)

Man will never be bored with his new freedom.
The thoughts and dreams of man, has
only scratched the surface of creation and
what God has to offer.

by
Lauresa Tomlinson
4/24/88

So Lonely Before

Creation is so lonely. As I watch the heavens, my attention is caught by a blue orb.

It is insignificant in the splendor of creation. I can't help but hold it in my grasp and bless it with the breath of life.

Gently I caress the surface and oceans form. Gently I breathe life upon the seas and pass my spirit upon the spreading life with each step.

Green abounds in my sight. I lovingly pause and take the fresh air into my lungs.

For compassion's sake, I breathe upon the lump of earth held in my hands and form man.

By
Laurence Tomlinson
1980's

Soaring High

Just like the stairway into the Heavens,
you lighten my day and
make my spirit soar like a bird of lofty heights.
You are the sunlight in my day and
the rainbow of my heart.
With you, I am as a cloud and as ageless
as the winds of time.
You are forever in my heart and thoughts,
Oh Holy Father of mine.

by
Lauresa Tomlinson
1981

Stepping Back

Step back is what I am told
Take another look, get a better hold

But the voice inside tells another tale.
Step to the side and let go,
Things change, don't run or bale.

Go with the flow, help guide when you can
Lend a helping hand, when asked
Time goes by, wanting or not, that's the plan

Learning, ever learning is the key
learning to love and get along
We are all Family, don't you see

Learning to Love yourself for who you will be
Everyone stumbles and sometimes falls
For if you don't love you, you can't love me

When you fall, which all of us have, get up
Brush it away with forgiveness and love
Get up, I say, today's a new day, drink from this cup

Looking behind you blinds you to your
next step forward
Live and Love for it's a new beginning
Look up and give thanks for this second chance
to go onward

by
Lauresa Tomlinson
5/90

The Fallen Goose

I went hunting, just last fall
Listened to the predator's call
Plenty of duck and Canadian geese
A gun I bought because no one would lease
Watch the sky I was quite intent
To bag a goose, figuring what I had spent
Into a slumber I fell, dead as a stone.
A wizard I met in my dream-filled state
Who didn't like hunting, and wanted to create
Someone who cared and cared with a passion
No mercy did he show but gave me a ration
Of magic words to discourage my zeal.
Then waved his hands, this couldn't be real.
I felt strange at first with a feeling of flight
Then looking down I found I was right...
Like water, the land flowed beneath me,
Master of the sky and all I could see.
Suddenly I felt pain as my breast blew apart
Something wasn't right, I knew in my heart.
Out of control, no longer flying free
Faster and faster the ground race to meet me,
My life past before me and the first thing I'd thought
Was that by an observant hunter I'd just been shot.
I awoke with a start and jerked with a wince,
Never will I hunt, I swore, and I haven't hunted since.

By
Laurence Tomlinson
1980's

The Fallen Goose 2

The Land flows like water beneath
Soaring above the plain
The wind is intense, invigorating
I hardly feel the pain
My body explodes from metal pieces
My speed begins to gain
Faster and faster the ground races to meet me
Over the sky I no longer reign

by
Laurence Tomlinson
1980's

To Swim - To Be - To Fly

To swim, to be, to fly as one with nature
Nature's thoughts and ours as one –
Then comes the answers to all our questions
Hopes that the wisdoms come with the
knowledge of the already known.
For only with love can Nature and
Humankind be helped.
For all was made one in the beginning
to work together as one.
Then can ego and the desire for power.
And even with all the power that man has today,
a small thing like air can undermine all of his greed
for power and selfishness.
So look at your goals and your reasons behind them
Are they leading you closer to nature and the
One who Created all that you experience?

by
Lauresa Tomlinson
1990's

The King Comes

It's been so dark so long, his chosen were but stars
In the midnight sky-
Waiting patiently for the angle's cry
YEAH!!
I'm glad I waited, Oh!
Yes I really am
All the suffering is over
It's time to see the Lamb

144 million and thousand, thousands ride-
Going into battle with armor made of light
Their time is now- to conquer and see the light
His chariot ride upon the lighting
His horsed are more brilliant than the sun-
They pull the King of King from his lofty heights

All Hail The King

It is forever day and never again night

The King is Coming   con't

I'm glad that I waited
Yes I really am
All the suffering is over
It's time to meet the Lamb

He's coming in the clouds
Everything laid low

Everything is trembling at His Mighty blow
YEAH!
I'm glad I waited
Yes I really am
All sufferings over
It time to see The Lamb

by
Lauresa Tomlinson
1983

We Are Students

To cry the muffled screams of pain and anguish of
the soul's trodden ways

To feel the suffering of times past and the hardening
grasp of reality on the spirit.

This is to experience life's side path

but to learn the lessons this master teacher is
the ordeal of man.

Be it now or later, these lessons must be learned

Be they fine and filled with laughter or pain,
they are the same.

To experience the experience is to live this life.

by
Lauresa Tomlinson
5/4/91

Who Are You?

Who are you? Are you what you see?
Are you who you show to others?
Are you who you really want to be?

Are you who your families wanted for you to be?
Are you really who you think you are?
Who are you?

Are you free?
Are you trapped by worry?
Are you trapped by anger, hate, or envy?

Are you trapped by hurts, doubts, debts, and karma?
Is freedom what you want, free to help others,
Free to be yourself, free to become one with the all?

Or are you trapped by
Wants and desires of ego and vengeance
Be freed by the one who loves so much
He gave his Only Son to show the way

He Created the love you can feel and
the happiness that abounds,
the freedom from all that binds.
Love with your whole being and
become who you really are.

by
Lauresa Tomlinson
9/28/94
inspired by music

To the Stars and Back

Well here I am, caught in the hues,
Which once were clear blue
Someone has awakened me
Now- could it have been you

Of all the vastness of space
You are the one that needed me most
Was caught in the mire of forgetfulness
But now awoke

I'm just one of the many who
Have been here before
Sent here to help you get to
Your reality's core.

The rest of like minds having
Spent time under control
Singing my song aloud,
Alert and quickened, I take a stroll

Time is mine to do what I want
And to help when I please
Sitting back smelling the flowers and
Feeling the cool breeze

To the Stars and Back　con't

Teaching time mastery to those who want
To become masters of their own reality

Time only masters those who pay it no mind
Then they later find themselves in a bind

For time is ours to have and to use
Not to set and abuse

So make yourself a peaceful place
in every time and space.
Enjoy it with those around you in
your own cozy place.

by
Lauresa Tomlinson
4/26/03

Truth??

In the heart of each of God's creation is
a portion of truth

Truth is like the grains of sand in the sea
each in itself does not make the beach

Only when all the grains are assembled together
does it make a whole

As it is with each portion of man's knowledge
One portion does not make the whole truth

Listen and gather as one does and
harvest the seeds of truth

Truth is only known when its knowing is
a whole part of creation

Only after putting each portion of knowledge together
with the wisdom of creation does man become
one with his Creator

If one Ask of Him,
let him receive the caring love of knowing

If one Seeks the knowledge –
let him learn the wisdoms of time

Truth??   Con't

Then come the Knowing and true life that
shines reflections of lights in the soul

Shine forth and show in love the kindness and
loving wisdom of The Creator.

by
Lauresa Tomlinson
5/3/88

You're my Sunshine

When I think of our love

It reminds me of the sunshine as it meets the beautiful
colored leaves on a magnificently shaped tree

Your smile reminds me of a sparkling rainbow as
it meets the shimmering fields of emerald green

I love you so very much

You are my sunshine and hope for tomorrow
Our love puts the silver lining in the blue clouds of life.

by Lauresa Tomlinson
1983

A little about one of the authors

Lauresa

    I was born in Oklahoma in 1947. I was trained to think for myself by my parents and grandparents, to never stop learning, because there would always be something more to learn. I am the mother of six children and change is the only thing that I have found to be a constant. I was taught to live as if I would pass from here in moments, but to plan for the future as if I would live 10,000 years. We have to learn to love ourselves if we ever plan to be loved. Even though sometimes we stumble, our next moment can be a second chance. After all is said and done Everyone is family.

Laurence

    He was born in San Francisco California. Lived in central CA most of his life. He met Lauresa in 1979 and they got married in 1981 and mover to Northern California a few years later.

A Collection of Love Sonnets and Thoughts

By
Lauresa Tomlinson
Larry Tomlinson

Why I Love You

I love you, not only for what you are but
for what I am when I am with you

I love you, not only for what you have
made of yourself but for
what you are making of me

I love you, for the part of me
that you bring out

I love you, for passing over all my
foolishness and weak traits that
you can't help but see

I love you, for drawing out into the light
my beauty that no one else
had looked quite far enough to find

I love you so very much for being you.

by
Lauresa Tomlinson
1980s

The Unicorn

Oh beautiful unicorn, you look so majestic standing among the flowers with your shimmering gold horn glimmering in the light and your brilliant white fleece shinning i the morning sun.

You, yes you, oh lovely one, Top the heights of my morning as I study your beauty and thank The Creator for doing such a surperb job in creating such splendor.

Through Time

Our love is as beautiful as sunshine when it touches the pines on an Autumn morning

As I look at the pine tree's reflection in the clearness of the pools lingering alongside the country stream, I see our love lingering throughout time for eternities as crystal clear and deep as a clear mountain pool.

As the country breezes drift across the beautiful wheat fields - so does time drift across our love for each other.

I love you darling

by Lauresa Tomlinson
1983

You're my Sunshine

When I think of our love

It reminds me of the sunshine as it meets the beautiful
colored leaves on a magnificently shaped tree

Your smile reminds me of a sparkling rainbow as
it meets the shimmering fields of emerald green

I love you so very much

You're are my sunshine and hope for tomorrow
Our love puts the silver lining in the blue clouds of life.

by Lauresa Tomlinson
1983

Loving You

Since you've come along
My life has changed in many ways
Dreaming of the time that I can spend
Holding you in my heart I know that feeling

Loving you forever and a day
each and every moment you are near
Makes me love more in every way

It's just time I'm taking
but I know it's right somehow
My heart is in need of rescue
I need you right now

Come take my hand
Together I can make it, you will see
Now my life is so completely filled
Having you here next to me

So I'll put my hands in yours
and I will make that climb
Loving you forever until the end of time

by Lauresa Tomlinson
1980s

Each day with you

My Love,
   As the sun sets, I see the gentle touch of your radiance in the glow of the clouds. The birds with their wind. Nature is quiet with anxiety as all the animals wait to see the wonders ahead of them, just beyond the stars. Just as I wait for the wonder and pleasures ahead with you. Each day, my love, I am more in love with you than I could conceive of the day before; as the bird Awake and Sees the Sun, Coming over the horizon.

I love you!!!

this sonnet was written on a card with two unicorns on it

Truth??

In the heart of each of God's creation is a
portion of truth
Truth is like the sand grains of the sea
Each in itself does not make the beach
Only when all the grains are assembled together
does it make a whole
As it is with each portion of man's knowledge
One portion does not make the whole truth
Listen and gather as one does in harvest the
seeds of truth
Truth is only known in its knowing, as a
whole part of creation
Only after putting each portion of knowledge
together with the wisdom of creation does
man becomes one with his Creator
If one Ask of Him, let him receive the caring
love of knowing
If one Seeks the knowledge –
let him learn the wisdoms of time
Then comes the Knowing and
rue life that shines reflections of
lights in the soul
Shine forth and show in love the kindness and
loving wisdom of The Creator.

by Lauresa Tomlinson
5/3/88

My True Love

Darling,

To a True man and the one that holds the Highest Place in my heart under God our Father

It is your love that I look forward to each morning. It's your arms and loving smile that helps to make my day. Having you close and feeling your love keeps me going when things in this world don't go according to plans.

I feel the verse in this card is true- "Nothing is so strong as gentleness; nothing so gentle as real strength" Indian Proverb

All yours with love

(inspired by a card- I wrote this inside)

So Happy
By
Lauresa Tomlinson

I am so happy when I'm with you.
Your turn my stormy times into shining stars
Our love lives in us for each other
like an endless rainbow.

Ever showing new ways of loving each other.
With every turn of life, I find my love for you
growing stronger and stronger.

I feel so relaxed when I'm with you.
So at ease just knowing you're nearby
when I need you.

No matter what happens in the world,
no matter what goes wrong or right,
in all that happens, our love for each other
is the only thing that remains constant.

1984

As I See You Now

As I stand here thinking of you and
the love we hold,
I see you in every turn teaching me to be bold

As the gull that flies free our love
soars to the heavens
Such love as ours is protected from
being shaken.

I hear your sweet voice in
the nightingale's song
And with every note
my heart sings along.

I feel your tender touch
as the warm summer breezes
It touches my skin and
givens me delicate squeezes.

I see your smiling face as the moon
looks down on me at night.
I see the love in your eyes through the
twinkling of the star's light.

I hold you in my arms all through
the night close to my heart

This way I keep you near even though
we are miles apart.

June 20, 1980

Your Gentle Touch
By
Laurence Tomlinson

    As the sun sets, I see the gentle touch of your radiance in the glow of the clouds. The birds with their heads buried under their wings. Nature is quiet with anxiety as all the animals wait to see the wonders ahead of them, just beyond the stars.
    Just as I wait the wonders and pleasures ahead with you. Each day, my love, I am more in love with you than I could conceive of the day before; as the birds awake and sees the sun coming over the horizon.

I Love you!!!
 1985

Sun Shine

Sun shine my darling, sunshine of my life
You make my heart sing with joy when
the rays of your beautiful love
shine on my soul

The love for me that shines
from your eyes set me free and
makes my soul sing with true happiness

When I bask in the sunlight of your love
my whole being soars with freedom
through the eons of time

I will love you past and
beyond the course of time

Through eternity our love will live and
prove love is the strongest thing ever created

Laurence Tomlinson
1987

Since I Found You

I am finding that each day with you is so beautiful
and outstanding that it is hard to explain.

My love for you has outgrown the vastness
of this universe.
You give me the love I had always dreamed of
as being perfect.

Between us, we hold the beautiful love that God had
always meant to be between a couple.

I love you so very much.
I have never stopped thanking God
for letting this, our meeting and
such a wondrous love that grew from it.

My Love

Darling,
　　　My love for you grows stronger each and every moment we are together. As a beautiful tropical flower grows and spreads its petals to show the beauty of life and love and the Glory of God, in its way helps to support life and that love we have that is so very strong.
　　　I enjoy life now more than ever since I found you, my whole life is alive and wonderful.

My Dearest Darling

    I am so very happy with you. I am so very much in love with you. It makes and keeps me very happy when I wake to your bright and loving eyes. You, my dearest darling, are my highest proclaimed Earthly love.
        The deepest part of my heart holds fast to your tender love for me.
    I feel like a Queen when I'm in your arms. My main dream in life was to have someone just like you to love me and to be able to make him happy beyond my earthly dream. Your my darling and only you could make the first part of my dream come true. Now my goal in life is to make your life as happy as mine is with you being your wife.

I love you so very much

Being Comforted

Darling,

    I see you as I see the kindness and beauty in the eyes of this unicorn. For when I'm in need of help, love, and understanding, you are always near to me.

    Being held in the loving warmth of your arms, nothing seems so bad.

    You seem to melt my worries into nothing with your loving-kindness. I see your beauty day in and day out and I thank God that he lets me be so lucky as to have a love so deeps as yours.

    I love you so very much. You and my children are my life.

    You are the only lover I have or ever want. My love for you grows with each and every day that goes around with this world.

I love you Darling

(note - this was in a beautiful card with a unicorn)

My Darling and Me

I love you so very much. If I was a flower I would choose you to be my bee and our children would be the honey of our love.

We go together like a soft white cloud in the light blue skies where the eagles fly high in the heavens

When the winds of time drift by us in the far future they will find us together

My love and me

Your Spirit

I love you so. Your Spirit is as impregnable and free as these two unicorns. Graceful, beautiful, and carefree your love encompasses all around you.

Your dreams are spacey and yet down to earth. You frolic to and fro much as these two do and are sensible about where and when you come down.

 I love you so much because you're you and no one, no one can change that!!!

by Laurence Tomlinson
1982

this sonnet was written of a
card with two unicorns on it

Sweet Love

My Darling,
    I sometimes forget myself and do something that doesn't agree with you. But I LOVE YOU no matter what!
    I love the twinkle in your eye, the curve of your thigh, as time goes by, HIGHER than HIGH, it makes me sigh, that you are my... Sweet Love.

Laurence Tomlinson
1990

Reality? Yours or mine

As I sit here on my bed, all snugly and warm watching the cold winter rain splash against my skylight, I wonder, reality? power? Just what does either of them have to do with life and the living. I mean every day at one point or another I have heard someone say, "Get back to reality". Don't they know that, what reality is to them, may or may not be reality to me. That is, just because they say the apple is red, doesn't mean the apple is red to me.

I may be thinking of the apple as being green or yellow. And who is to say that the words I use for saying something is red isn't the same as the ones someone else uses to say isn't green. I agree with what Shakespeare was saying when he said, a rose by any other name.... So maybe words, aren't the real or right way to communicate. I'm thinking that if... when I speak to you I send groups of pictures instead of words, then you would know just what I was trying to get across. And neither of us would get turned around on words and their meanings, which can lead off into new thoughts and problems and soon the thought begins conveyed is lost by the wayside.

I have to further say that I enjoy talking to people that put their ideas and thoughts across to me in the form of pictures When I talk to them it's like watching a short film. It is very entertaining and I understand exactly what they are trying to get across by the time we are through talking

Power? Now that is a word that gets a lot of use and abuse. We have people in this world who are hungry for power over other people. Life for them just isn't worth living unless they can rule what others think, do, or say. Each of us has power, it is given to us at birth, no matter what rank or area we are born into. And, yes, If you are working for someone other than yourself to earn money, then you will have to do things the way they want them done during the hours you are working for them.

When you are in the service of someone else, just making sure that the work you are doing is not going against your own judgment because at that point you are giving away your power. You have power over your life and the way you live it. All you have to do is ask for your purpose to become apparent.

by Lauresa Tomlinson
1992's

These are the few of the most meaningful poems and sonnets that have made it through the fires, floods, thief's and moves we have made through the many years we have been together here.
   We have found that true love never dies or gets misplaced. It is one of the strongest bonds that the Holy Creator of our existence has made.
   Always enjoy what you have and lookup for more of the good things to come.

   Happiness to all and may true love bless all that you touch.

   Lauresa Tomlinson
   2018

Other Books by Lauresa Tomlinson

The Turning Stone
My Interview With a Fairy
There's an Alien in My Cereal
Munchie and Goldie – Most Unlikely Friends
Cats in Charge
Sleepy Time Baby Bear
Secretly Special – You May be Special too
Elaytay's Adventures in Space and Time
(part one) We Came to Visit
(part two) We Meet at Last
(part three) Which Time May Be
Crazy Deja Vu (pt one)
Crazy déjà vu – Not Again
Expressive Tree People

In the future
Magic Under the Pear Tree (companion of Interview)
The Whirling Worlds of Kanisia
Too many cats
Five Little Friends
Spud, Bud and the Magic Mirror
Rubumps

Group of stories

Few Things Change, Almost a Prince,
Wild Woman Pie, Lonely Little Tree,
Ever Wonder If?

www.ingramcontent.com/pod-product-compliance
Lightning Source LLC
Chambersburg PA
CBHW050203130526
44591CB00034B/2080